I0531761

SHOES FOR BABY

STEVE SIBRA

Copyright © 2022 Steve Sibra

Shoes for baby

ISBN-13: 979-8-9853120-1-0 (Print)
ISBN-13: 979-8-9853120-0-3 (eBook)

All rights reserved. No part of this publication may be reproduced, distributed, or transmitted in any form or by any means, including photocopying, recording, or other electronic or mechanical methods, without the prior written permission of the publisher, except in the case of brief quotations embodied in critical reviews and certain other noncommercial uses permitted by copyright law.

For permission requests, write to the publisher, addressed "Attention: Permission Requested," at the address below:

Swallow Publishing, LLC
937 Northwest 83rd Drive
Coral Springs, Florida
33071

For more information visit **www.swallowpublishing.com**

This book is dedicated to Ayesha Siddiqa

تمام گانے آپ کو واپس آجائیں گے

And to the memory of my first mentor Lawrence B. Green

Table of Contents

II

IV

Shoes For Baby: An Introduction by Erika Brumett

Trickster? Philosopher? Lover? Imp? Attempt to pin down this poet, then spin and spin and spin. *Shoes for Baby* rouses an array of voices, in a range of tones. From a least weasel to Mary Shelley, "most of them are hauntings," summonings, visitations evoking "the ghost of a story/ or the story of a ghost." And while speakers shift shape with each invocation, this collection could only have been conjured by Steve Sibra.

By Steve Sibra, alone in his kitchen at 3:00 am. Beside him, a glass of whiskey on a stack of drafts. A cat. Here are poems from those pre-dawns, from those madman romps when the rest of us slept. Here are poems as resistant to categorization as the poet, himself. That said, throughout the book, play is always at work. Sibra delights in twists of narrative, absurdities of character, frisking stanza to stanza with a puckish bliss. He offers us talking animals, sisters who kiss, "Five Fickle Uses for Pickle Juices," a future where human breath replaces elevator music.

Yet revelry extends beyond the level of story. Sibra invites readers to carouse in sound. "Wedding Soup," for instance, serves up a sonic wit, delicious despite its ingredients, "dumped/ into the caldron/ under rose hips,/ some loud person's lips." Again and again, this spirit of play toys with word-choice, cavorts with voice, enjoys the comical by way of the musical. Sibra writes each line like a lifeline, vibrating and alive -- "I hold an insect to my lips./ I sing into its dream."

Free-at-play does not, however, mean free-of-pain. *Shoes for Baby* aches as it capers. These pages throb and rollick, repeatedly sketching death erotic. In "Scabbard," a female narrator slays with a male dagger, discovers relief (release?) as she buries her blade into a sheaf. Indeed, burials abound: someone's beloved rots in a relic-box, while an ear hears from underground.

But deeper still — below those (often jocose) reposes — lies a quieter anguish. A more honest assessment of mortality. A hurt so direct and intense, its loneliness must be expressed through subtext -- "Nothing but cold cuts/ and a longing to forget." Here, Steve asks readers to enter his screen-lit, 3:00 am kitchen. This request is not from neediness, but from an awareness he has much to teach us. About the clock, how hours aren't ours. And about suffering, how "there is rhythm/ in what is lost."

So go on in. Sit a while beside him.

Preamble: Tales of Ivory

Beneath the gray dome of winter,
I write stories. Most of them are hauntings,
pale, quiet along the periphery
screaming like dying giants inside my skull.

The ghosts are always whales
alive in oceans of the metaphysical
ethereal and immense
humpback, sperm
filtering their tiny words
through a sieve of flesh and blood.

My best conversations,
with pictures on milk cartons –
not just lost souls, but animals,
sheep, mostly, or cattle
grazing in fields of confusion
writing poetry in the grass
with their grinding jaws.

Milk carton creatures are ghosts
as well, written by a giant
hand of tragedy.
I cannot claim or absolve them,
only punish myself with their sorrows.

Everyone and everything I know
or do, every tear drying on my skin
is the ghost of a story, or the story
of a ghost, some essential enamel
extracted from the jawbone of a God
of Words. My tears are His tears,
my thoughts are fires lit inside
the whale I have been swallowed by,
precious oxygen needed to live --
instead, I burn it in the dwindling,
futile flame of a story.

SECTION 1

IN A BOWLING BALL FIGHT, THERE ARE NO WINNERS

MINERVA, BORN INSIDE THE WIND

(A Savage Least Weasel Named Minerva Speaking with an Old and Tired Domestic Named Oberon)

Come now,
    Look at me, I am floating
    see how my slim bones bend
    I am as green as a sapling, a tiny
    willow, only now a new sprout –
    only now born into the hollow of the wind.

Look at you,
    Twisting slow like some dying thing,
    almost invisible under tall beards of barley
    you have wisdom, I know you do
    you can pull yourself from the grip
    of yellow black mud. I know
    you are simply an old barn cat, beaten down,
    you no longer see colors, I know
    you no longer love the light.

Rise to embrace,
    No one knows how long you have laid fallow,
    lost to the humans, lost to the wild
    how long sleeping alongside the dead
    pieces of life that came before, bird
    skulls, vertebrae, husks of empty wings –

wings silent in the death which I delivered,
a bed where you have slept and wept.

Reawaken, open your body.
    Make the wind your own as you fly,
    create a world just yours and mine,
    we swoop and soar, taking coup
    we rip open brains like vicious scholars
    leafing madly through an essential text,
    tearing out, consuming crucial passages,
    yearning, learning, putting to use.

INTO THE WILD

we close our eyes
feel the membranes quiver
our hair suggests seaweed --
with depth of breath
comes chipped chorus
of ancient bells

We step into the wild,
uplifted not through the physical --
but noises, chants of cicadas
disenchanted

palms fold inside a globe --
water's innocence
like prayers, slow to rise,
halo of the afterglow --
thoughts thicken
a dull scissors cuts
beautiful skin

SOMETHING'S GOT TO GIVE

Now this one here, my uncle,
eyes narrowing,
has always been a real bitch
for an old man to open without help.

Slams down the accelerator,
Dodge three-quarter ton gallops
through barbed-wire gate, my hands
bone white against the dash

wires snake through the air like horsewhips,
I hear a corner post snap off,
sheared like a cotter key. Truck

bucks to a halt. He sits, weathered
leather behind the wheel

looks like you got fence to fix, he grins
teeth yellow from cigarettes
and swallows of sin.
Be sure to leave slack
in the pull, so an older man
don't have to give up his dignity
getting to the other side.

UNTITLED #3

Sitting in tall grass
between midnight
and summer's last gasp,
I hold an insect to my lips –
I sing into its dream.

Electricity of my voice,
creature begins to sing
along -- clicks and scrapes
of its thorax, it makes me
want to quit this copper
tinted land, swim through dust
and maple leaves, turn
a sea of sky to gold,
unfold metal wings
lift off, fly a thousand heartbeats
inside my insect chest.

Sitting in tall grass
between midnight
and summer's last gasp,
an insect holds me to its lips

TREPANATION

"a surgical intervention in which a hole is bored or scraped into the human skull"

1.
In the glory of the Opening
we have learned so much,
we know now --- total darkness
is not total, that which is absolute
is not absolute, there is no truth
so untruthful as a declaration
of complete extremity.

When rain falls, it falls –
when there is cessation of rain,
still the cool air remembers,
still the wetness on the skin,
water travels in to and then
from the eyes.

All acts of power must be
ritualized. No other process
legitimates strength. Proof
is only proof of the moment,
it has no life of its own.
If you prove me wrong, one second
later I am right once more.
A door which swings, swings –

Thou shalt not unhinge your heartbeat
from the chest's red, wet core.

Purity of aperture borne of the drill,
it mitigates the pain
like the ceaseless patter
of remembered rain.
In time it drops you off,
you might miss it, or forget
yet it will not lose sight of you.

2.
What the pagan forgets,
is the tenacity of the Creator.
He is in the habit of control, some
call it guidance, but it is rarely so gentle
as that. If His nature is to create,
why would he create man, and then stop?

It makes no sense. It is not what you
would do, or me, or any sane being.
He has more work to do
for me, for you, for Himself
most of all.

Like any who creates, there must
also be the endless tinker.
That which is made, is to always
be improved upon. Creation

is perpetual motion, a building
forever rebuilding itself.

If Enlightenment is the goal,
we must make a pathway
in. We must open the door
for Him, make him comfortable,
let Him do the work
for which He created himself.

THE STRANGER

Second I saw him.
side of the road, I knew.

"I love you", I said.
As he turned, I struck him,
a mallet breaking excuses.

He folded
    like a wallet of stars,
my fist a rock inside him –
a punch, a beating,
the call of a second heart.

We lay down together,
side of the road –
brotherhood,
strangest of battles.

BUTTE MORNING

Atop the Rocky Mountains, at one of the high points in the Continental Divide, stands a ninety-foot-tall statue of the Blessed Virgin Mary, overlooking the town of Butte, Montana.

No matter how early they rise,
Our Lady of the Rockies has already set the table.
It's the breaking of a wicked fast
for the lost angels
looking to cleanse their spirit
in the yellow Berkeley Pit runoff
of Butte Silver Bow County.

There is a hardness in the air,
morning sun ricochets off concrete -
sidewalk rough underfoot,
jagged
like broken bones pushing through skin.

This city fills with empty men,
their home travels with the sun across the horizon.
In the old bus station,
walls feel themselves crumbling.
Bum sings a Barry Manilow song
calling out to lost love,
someone buried in the mines of memory.

Men without pants piss
in dark corners, laughter
louder than the splash of release.
Everyone about at this hour
some kind of mongrel dog –
forsaken even by themselves
due to excess and absence.

The hopeless have abandoned each other here.
There is so little to redeem,
when the dead eyes of the man next to you
become your only mirror.

Like some wastrel oasis,
grim shadows open wide
onto sunshine at the entrance on Harrison.
By the curb, remnants of the strip miner brunch –
half-eaten chocolate bar,
crumpled soda can, filterless Camel
and a spent condom.

Eight thousand feet above the sea,
Our Lady wearies of gray chains
of earth and sorrow.
She lifts her gaze
above the clouds, along the Big Sky –
so clean, so clear,
such a limitless shade of blue.

SECTION 2

IS IT LAUGH? IS IT SNEER? THE FUN HOUSE MIRROR

THE FUTURE

In the future everyone will get over
themselves at the same time.
No one will have anything
to say about it. In the future
the past is past tense. Sound
of people breathing

replaces music in elevators,
meditation is the new temper
tantrum. Inside public restrooms,
in corn fields people sit,
backs straight as fallen arrows.

It's a new time, a new place
a world has popped its cork
boys suffer scratchy monkeys
in their copper codpieces
and girls grow to fifteen feet

In the future fuzzy dice from a rear
view mirror is an automatic life
sentence, refreshments provided
at the hearing, ice cream or gumballs.

In the future new days are dawning
around every corner, so much

to talk about, everything gets
said twice – once in words,
later when witch doctors scatter bones.

IT'S JENNIFER

charges truck stop counter
like a crazy diesel
skinny mixed-up world
I watch her walk
devil on her hip
she loads slim dancer flesh
stacks a stool
"It's Jennifer!" she yells
outside birds explode from trees

J. tugs on heartstrings
fiddles hair
orders plate of eggs
her pitch is farm fresh
when she makes an "O"
you hear the vulvas pop
she sits cross-legged
little Goth sidewinder
gulps my pizza
chugs ketchup from the bottle
stool's squeak so shrill
she swivels hips
typhoid merrily goes round
blows up natural order

"It's Jennifer" I whisper
as air leaves the room
my roll of quarters
going through the change
she sweeps back
black curtain of hair
reveals pale tender mouth
wolfs eggs
then off to marry a lawyer

WEDDING SOUP

some sort of white
flesh, ripped from the chest
of a galloping chicken,
slathered in black
tar tomato paste
some peas sneezed
prodded from the pod
unpeeled potato
stomped like a monkey's
red rump, dumped
into the cauldron
under rose hips,
some loud person's lips –

a smoldering habanero,
powdery lemon
zest, as a testimony
to the unexpected --
anoint it with waters
of love, sacrifice --
boil it for eternity.
Spoon onto one
another's soft, sweet
tongues, hold it
between lip and gum,
swallow once,

now twice –

swear a sacred vow

to be nice.

THE LADIES OF YAKIMA

All Hail the Ladies of Yakima!
Blonde 80s hair frames chipmunk cheeks
puffy with Corn Nuts and red meat malice
angel hair pasta spills from butcher shop eyes.

Watch now as they ride to challenge
Rodeo Queens of Ellensburg,
domain of Eastern Washington State hangs in the balance.
Yakima hips bounce like horseback pinatas,
migrant workers flee in terror in the face
of the saddlebags of sugary goodness.

Aftermath eye shadow drips like river mud.
It crawls between your toes
as the Ladies sit at your feet.

Glue-on lashes slather the air
with Butterball turkey fat.
Imagine that! They slice through
September sky like windmill blades.

Wild woman breath
like a car crash on the back of your neck,
air fills with spurs that jingle jangle --
they ride now for Wenatchee
to splatter the apple orchards with pine tar mascara

and crippled baby bird sweat that slides along
scarred crevice between their breasts.

It's a salty roller coaster ride
with a wrecking ball finish
to rival the Senior Center Easter Breakfast
in Union Gap
if you can picture that.

STRANGE WOMEN OF THE OCCULT

They fear everything
each other, most of all
cry out in twilight
spells to crack the sky
attack old enemies
over rivalries forgotten
or imagined, turn each other's
husbands to wood
make black cats
begat white pups
reverse perverse incantations
twist bad people into good

all night long, throw bones
against pale church walls, chant
in low tones, break crystal balls
pitch black stones down dry wells
bewitch one another with spells,
speak in tongues
breathe poison potions
into ancient lungs

On Sunday morning all break
bread, apologize for lightning
bolts shot through head, even pause

to laugh or cry, regret old hexes

wonder why

THE EYEBALL

The eyeball has a liberal texture,
free as wet leather
chaps, water running long-
legged like a guzzle
onto a floor covered in hay,
the eyeball walks with
the world hanging on,
swinging by threads. The eyeball

nestles on a raft of soft toast
where less is more, it
floats in porcelain repose
of its own contours. A nod
to necessity, ringing like gnats
in giant ears, hands
flailing to swat everything away,
slam it home --
force it to smile,
coiled beneath the weight
of violence, set to music

the eyeball waits to cry
until timid flesh sleeps,
it has more
important lives to lead --
what you see is not

what you get --
what you see

is what gets you.

.

CHICKEN ON THE GROUND

In the town of Eden, North Carolina, a security camera captured the early morning explosion of a KFC restaurant, launching a ball of flame and recognizable chicken parts.

"When life was finger-lickin' good and God lived in our
neighborhood
At them old campground meetin's eatin' chicken on the ground."
-gospel song

Breast; thigh
drumstick beat against tender sky –
big three soar, no matter
bake or fry – the Colonel's world erupts
crisp, bite-size morsels; fatty coating
midst hapless hens emoting
flightless fowl that spring from grill;
wings reach heights unheard
for such a useless bird
while the fleshy leg lags; lacks
both altitude and attitude
and brown skin peels from bony backs.
Whenever dead chickens fly
corncobs and Cole slaw in paper sacks
beans baked too wet, spuds mashed too dry
still in style after all these years --
choice white meat draped in white suits

poultry bodies brought down to ground
dark meat trampled without sound
while ghosts like feathers fly.

DECEMBER UNDER BROKEN WINDOWS

In the winter months, I was your father,
even though I possessed no gender,
even though my attachments were carved of wax.

I drew you in with my aura of misery,
it was nectar to your bumblebee. My stones
cradled in your chambers as organs pumped.

In your hunger you bit the heads
from nestled sparrows, assuring me:
"do not worry, they are made of chocolate"

On our outing the river wore a skin
of ice. To please you I waded in,
stood with the pain until my ankles
snapped. You laughed, called me
a skate, with the wind catching
my ears like throttles.

I never had a child of my own,
just bouncing season to season –
you with dead birds in your eyes,
never giving cause for alarm.

We used one another like flesh
combusting, a long December

under broken windows,
pistons in search of cylinders.

SECTION 3

SLEEPWALKERS

SLEEPWALKER

As we slumber,
skeletons slip through skins
march green-eyed
over dead moon lawns

unaware, we snore on
visions of elephants
and accidents, stolen
wallets jammed
with broken dreams

morning drops
from an orange sky
our sleeping bodies
stretched over damp soil

in the lavender graveyard
we open our eyes

LIGHTNING

I used to fear it
until the day it struck
me in an open field,
spun me high into the air
like circumstance, I flew
above the power lines,
a glimpse into the basement
windows of Heaven:
laid low in the dirt. Finding
myself one with the electric
birds who always fly too high
for the human eye to see,
now they dive inside
my purple skull, chasing broken
threads of memory,
circling my brain like rain
clouds eager to wash away
dreams I had scattered like offspring,
before there was light
or dark
or world

WE DREAM OF MORNING

Soft the music plays.
The King of the Dead
raises one hand
above his head,
he kills us in our beds
as we dream of morning –

soft come our sighs,
we close our eyes
roll over onto our sides –
our bones turn to ash,
gray canals within our souls
as flesh collapses unto flesh
and the air –

so cold.

THE LETTERMAN

There's a dead guy hanging
in downtown bars, he's haunting
my letterman's coat, wearing
cream and red colors
girls think he is the top
in pops, he signs my autograph
slops drinks down their shirts
they laugh, nudge his dead shoulder
they think he is me, just wiser
just older, just tanner, blonder,
bolder -- makes me wonder
which part of my impending corpse
has he crawled out from under?
What words he speaks
come from my tongue, air
so long dead inside my lungs?
How long have I held it,
how deep in the puddle must I sink,
before my conscience decides
to swim? There is a dead guy
haunting downtown bars, my red
and cream letterman's coat
covers all his scars, everybody
loves him, if I touch him
with broken, tattered fingers
am I a dead man as well?

Am I just an afterthought,
a feeling which lingers?
If the dead guy downtown
is really me, am I looking down
from Heaven or up from Hell?
He is doing a good job,
I am not sure it matters.

THING AS MIDNIGHT

from a conversation with Ayesha Khan

No such thing as midnight
did you know?

The night is a globe
a center with no edge

Night is a curtain without end
or dimension, it emerges

like the sea – to speak of the sea
as a thing with front or back

beginning or middle is pointless
sea or night   each is a nothing

made from a limitless number
of everythings – it is the sea

It is night -- it is your face
in my mind. Right now.

EARTHBOUND

ASK within a cold dream / reSpond with woRdS

little lady
of light
tattoos
by moon
bind your
passion's
wing   break
gravity's vein

gravitas
a collage of thrones

barbs of a heart
valentine's day
gone astray
to space you
are so hard

wired with
ruins of sanity
contemplate
a gate between
as you push

tides to shore

feathers

of morning

wearing

your globe

like a slide

eye of night

slippery

as ice

cream crowns

A.S.K

SECTION 4

A FARMER'S HANDS ARE HIS BIBLE

GRANITE COUNTY WEDDING DANCE

The women fought like gobbling turkeys,
trying to rip out each other's ovaries with their words.

Bride's father danced naked from the hips up, tipsy
drunk on promises of failing reputations,

Boots clicking like crickets on hard dirt platform --
everyone yipping at spits of oil from the rusty grill,

where chicken necks sizzled like loose-tongued gossip
soaked to the throat in gopher drippings.

Uncles and aunts traded off pairs of pants
bosses bossing posse above furrowed dirt.

Whistles made from old soup cans cut us
shrill, all the insects fell, turning over

onto their slick black backs. A dead man
tied girls' braids in sheepshank knots,

in open air on a distant farmstead
we did not care what daylight had seen,

across the big sky moon shined bright
if we knew nothing, the moon knew our names –

we understood the moon.

BUSTING SOD

Break open the earth
gashes ripped in the crust

rocks surface
like blood clotting

we pile them high
home for the rattlers

who sleep wide
in white shadow

a funeral of stone

A WORKMAN CONTEMPLATES HIS TOOLS

Hands of a working man,
a history book at arm's length

each day's effort carves
deeper lines, each line

holds new words, some
of wisdom, a few of shame

the hands open slowly, like a venerable tome -
sturdy, yet creased by the weight of their labors

in his palms, the psalms
so gravely earned, so precious

he need not bother to read them,
he knows each line by heart

PRAIRIE LIGHT

My room has four east windows,
one for each Beatle
as I spin 45s at six-thirty
a.m. on a Tuesday, summer
of sixty-seven. An eleven-
year-old cross-legged on linoleum,
I want this to be the lotus position
but I do not know what that is,
what it means, what I am doing
with my life of Liverpool dreams,
whistling along to George's
sitar, I am only thinking
about the light outside my windows
not the light in the room, how
it comes from inside me, swan's
egg opening onto the world,
for just a moment, I know all,
I feel all, there in the room
with me, and then my mother
her voice on the stairs

WHY MICE DO NOT LIKE PEPPERMINT

As with all worthwhile questions,
the answer is in the Farmer's Almanac –
a wet moon tips out the rain
a dry eye shines
into the constellation's brain. Sometimes
too strong –
pleasure times a hundred
equals pain, the peppermint
hell of sadness
tingles holes in your heart.
Peppermint pleases and poisons
with a single taste.

COULEE'S BOTTOM

Tonight,
trapped in the cage of your own humanity,
Death puts her song inside of you.

It's not far.
Listen to the sound
imprisoned by wind.

Soft chains of comfort
paralyzed by a civilized mind.

You lie in your distant bed,
stars drain from the sky,

spread to a field of terror –
calls from the pack
in agony.

Splitting the icy stream
at Coulee's Bottom
hind feet bitten in a frozen trap,

coyote cub wails.
Wind drums the arctic air.

TOP OF THE HILL, THEN DANA ROAD

and suddenly she is there
like the spirit of an old fisherman
arms pinwheel   above her head
her hat is knit from old beer cans
she points as we approach

memory is a ghost
a dish served hot over kindness
thin slices of a friendly time
a good haunt as wheels
slow and we turn in

plateful of the present
a world of confusion
sadness   disappointment
reality of the here and now
nothing but cold cuts
and a longing   to forget

SECTION 5

LOVE, A DOG BARKING, A BELL IN A DISTANT TOWER

SCABBARD

She was delighted to have it available to her. She needed a
repository, a solid space out of the sunlight in which to keep him
when she was not plunging him into beating hearts. Inside it smelled
like dirt and lavender. It was lined with animal hairs. Sometimes it
was leather, cracking and obtuse. Other times it was made of chains.
It folded in upon itself with rhythm. It was the sound of gravity
letting go.

TRAPPINGS

Folded up inside a chair
I fell asleep   when I
awoke   no one was
there   I was alone

I found a single strand
of your jet-black hair
long and luxuriant
like an animal napping

in the sun   I dozed
once more the mist
of our love sleeping
inside you

your naked arm
stretched bare across my chest
it was so dark
I could not see your face

short stiff bristle
peppered my tongue
salt of the earth

FEATHER PILLOW

I close my eyes
she rains through my bedroom
window   I pick up
a feather pillow, place it like an ocean wave
beneath her toes
she steps light without speaking
props me up straight as a surfboard
inside her storm.

THE WHITE WIDOW

Sit back, light the White Widow
she burns for your kiss
embrace her like whiskey lips
It's the merchant marine thing to do,
time of day draws like autumn and ice cream
fresh, remember to slow the spin
don't stop until you taste her love
on your tongue, she comes
in bitter, goes out sweet
or is it the other way around

ETCHINGS

she lays down
to nap   he is there
long blade shimmering

she closes
her eye   night begins
he slices through

her bloodless skin
breathes   arcs her body
of work   lines of crayola
thrift shop vermillion
wax flowing like tiny
plasma rivers he begins

in no time
slivers of her   spread
to the sea   everywhere

wind becomes light
made white

echoes of laughter

TELL ME WHAT WE WANT

do we connect?
are we peas in pods?

are there dents matching dents in our foreheads?

is the sky a limit?

is there love after war?
do we make blonde love inside a tent on the front lines?

do you need breakfast between the sheets?

is there love after war?
does the Big Lie defy the Big Secret?

are there hollow speeches to be made?

is there prayer?

do you cry yourself to sleep each night?
do you miss the things we never had?

did you build this fire to be so cold?

WHEN SHE KISSES HER SISTER

She does not know how she got here,
so deep in this dark forest
of grinding hips and peppermint lips.

She can taste it. A cat
with sandpaper tongue
kneading her claws into another's breast.

Love is old as the bald hills;
it's grand like a golden canyon,
beautiful as a broken piano.
Music of love is strange,
uncomfortable and colorful pain.

Music is a kiss on the face of forbidden
objects. The subject is bound
to object; you have to hear
"Yes yes yes" when the natural ear
hears "no no no."

AUGUST PASSING

breakfast crowns
plastic cup, diced peaches
old cottage cheese
like Sahara on the tongue

window frames my dog
he does as all dogs do
while a master watches
behind glass

Summer mornings drop
long and let none rest
even blackbird's beak
spent shouting down
sparrows who swoop
mock the empty nest

each morning this summer
I compose a letter
to my dead mother,
when push comes to shove

I lay down the law
get her off my back
out the door
never gone or for good

as white sun rises
crows tear skin from peaches
in the trees. Somewhere
to the south cicadas

sleep with one eye open
farmer belches, drops red
onions into a sack
his wife begged him

for a child, now
he piles bags of onions
on her grave, he pretends
she eats them
pink ripening into yellow
like candied fruit

I FORGOT YOU

I forgot your existence.
I was in the basement
of my soul, working
with my hands,
holding things of small and large
consequence, unmindful
of things too large, too small
to fit those hands.

You are too large to fit in my hands
and too small to fit in them, as well
you are buried so deep in an ocean
of emotion, I cannot reach down
pull you back to surface
you are a pair of wings so tiny,
so distant into the realm of stars
gray clouds stifled by tears
weave beneath your bare feet

You are naked to me always,
invisible behind curtains made of
some other season on some other world
I forget you as if you were my breath
moving in and out, as if you were
a gentle heartbeat

the way salt forgets pepper's
gentle nip

I forget you as life and death
forget time, as the sun
forgets its own shine.

FILLING A CAVITY

A month after my father
died, I slipped on the ice
on his doorstep

broke out a front tooth
on cold concrete. At the dentist
I opened wide, he gazed in

for a long moment, I waited.
"Through the gap," he told me,

"I can see into Eternity.
Your father is there
like a photograph

from forty years ago, biceps
bulging inside a white t-shirt,
tiny kitten in his arms."

Knowing it was wrong to fix
a thing so plainly unbroken,
I left the office, went to the shelter

picked out the smallest, most frail
animal I could find. Together
we went home, to spend our days

purring, rubbing each other's
cheeks, eyes closed, eating only
soft foods, gazing out the window
as winter slipped into the green

GRAND CANYON DIVORCE

he wonders how much weight
can a body carry   how much
flesh to leave behind floating
like a raven's feather

he sits as if the nothing
beneath his feet   solid
as a wish   or pools
of silver   winds coming up
from the bottomless drain
play his song   legs dangle

she loves him still   just enough
foot on the gas   never looks back
from raging fires below   warm airs rise

RED CURRY

She comes to me, red curry
on a bed of onion skin,

she has sparkles, sprinkles,
she is spicy hot and thin:

cumin, ginger, coriander,
turmeric, all sit within

presses herself to my lips
I open up, welcome her in

SECTION 6

MY PAPA, HE MADE ME A FRANKENSTEIN

I PLAYED MY GUITAR IN THE BATHROOM TODAY

I missed you today
as I have each day since you've gone
I ring the doorbell to hear it scream
bloody murder, carrots in the fridge
think the walls are funhouse mirrors –
pulled teeth have taken root
in caragana bushes, Russian olives
grow branches through cracks like skeleton arms.

You called this place a dead end,
smell of rotting flesh in the Coppertone
kitchenette, where garbage is piled high.

I sit all day inside my melancholy,
your words stand in memory on my chest
like free weights, they hold me down.
That morning when you told me you were going,
I tried to let it be. Inside the kitchen drawer,
sharp objects made pointed arguments --
they bayed like hounds
with a moon in the middle
and a lavender tabletop that shined
with a bounce of the light in your eye.

I played my guitar in the bathroom today
where you lie under floorboards

your good ear turned upward
and your knees in your face.

It's a sad song
one we both used to know
I will play it again for you
when the spring roses knock
at the sliding glass door
bearing white petals to sprinkle
on new bright crimson floors.

ARK

A skeleton
hanging
from a sycamore
tree

in my back yard
each time
I look for it
I see

It turns gentle
on tiny
breeze
sun, season
grays the bone

no one
else can see
I know
it comes for me

it is a vessel
ship on a sea
it bides its time
like a bride for me

when the moon ripens
I must climb inside
to rule or ruin
I will ride

THE ICE CREAM DREAMING OF WEASEL MONAHAN

Some mornings he wakes up
and he's just not there.

His father listens to country music,
and loves the color orange. He beats
Weasel's mother with a passion
she cannot leave the house
for days because of the signs.

She says she knows it's wrong,
but it makes him calm.

Weasel dreams his father
is not real, or is a zombie,
or a mummy, or a cartoon.
His father takes him
to high school football games,
swears at referees and coaches,
hopes Weasel will someday play.

Weasel dreams even when awake,
of ice cream slides on a playground

buried in a pit, far below
his father's house, where monsters
sit and smoke and watch

their children running in the dark,
laughing, eating each other's faces.

LET THE JAMAICAN FRANKENSTEIN

Let the Jamaican Frankenstein
sigh as he runs his thick stubby digits
down your spine, then up through your wisps
of blonde hair. Dying fireflies
pile their bodies at your feet
shine their fading glow upon the apples and oranges
that line the pathway from the forest
to your humble trailer park hovel

Your hands grasp the stained pressed wood walls
as the soup ladle rattles in the pot
let the Jamaican Frankenstein explore
your limits, your regions of dark synthesis
and cold fear
once frozen now a monster sparked into life
and all the worse for it

The devil's tinny voice
comes across the hollow radio speaker
rattling like a rock in the hubcap
on your child's broken red wagon

Cry out to the gods and their kingdoms of filth
goats of despair in their winter coats
while the Jamaican Frankenstein knits
his dreads along your soft inner thigh
snakes of legend and the smoky taste

of human flesh on your tongue

Is it your own? Or a remnant

from the patchwork beast's earlier conquest

sewn into the sofa cushions

then joyously torched

A BABY FOR FREE

They brought me here blindfolded,
this town is like no place
ever, everybody who comes
is king, they red-carpet you
each and every person can go
to any door and knock --
they give you a baby for free

No questions or rules, nobody asks
to see an ID, they all have seaweed
hanging from hooks in entryways.
They reach in like a presto rabbit
out of a hat, they hand you a brand new
a real live baby for free, imagine that.

Paperwork well it is minimal,
I mean it's a baby, it belongs to you,
go ahead - name it anything
you choose, name your baby
Frankenstein – there is nothing
more beautiful, a brand new,
shiny wet seaweed baby.

THE WOMAN IN THE BOX

"Twenty-six-year-old Colorado bride suffers stroke, dies while
dancing at the party after her wedding."

Each touch of wind; a lung
like bellows through a skeleton
bones turned yellow under a torrent
of tears. Once a year
he opens her up
lets a fly scrape its heels in her dust
razor legs rub
scrub twelve months as tiny bits of rust
drift into blonde white detail.

The lace, the gown all but gone,
lost now forever her modesty's tint
he cannot bear to touch
her last wisps of hair
too brittle to withstand the brush
too fragile for the rustling air.

Each year on the anniversary of their beginning
he cracks both windows first
before unveiling her boarded throne;
he creates a passing breeze
to watch as gentle winds reanimate
the world he so longed to live in,

now driven, like his madness

into a simple box of unforgiven bone.

THE OLD ADMIRAL DETECTS A STRANGE ODOR

Darling, it's so stuffy in this house,
couldn't we open it up a touch in here?

And such a sour look upon your face; let me
get the tincture and a dropper, let's sweeten you

a bit. Your eyes – they seem filmy, like cake frosting
on cathedral windows. You poor thing.

How about after tea, we nip out to the barn, where
the blowflies gather in grimy window panes,

I will grab them by the handful, cup your mouth --
you can gobble them down, to get your meat.

MY SICK KITTY

I have a sick kitty
Her heart has turned to stone
I rake my teeth along her spine
To make a purring sound.

Her eyes still twinkle brightly
Though she never turns her head
Her fur? A bit unsightly
Some have dared to say, "She's dead."

But they don't know my kitty
Or see that sparkle in her eye
When the midnight wind blows softly
I can almost hear her cry

WALK A CROOKED PATH TO THE STRAIGHT AND NARROW

Cottonwood Lake squatted like a ruptured duck
tickle to the toes of Crazy Mountain. *And another thing*
my sister said, as we carved up Stepfather's body
Never wash raw chicken before cooking it

We submerged the monster's parts,
took a fervent if not sacred vow,
kissed one time, long and slow –
began the steep hike back to civilization

Sometimes hard work is its own reward
she said, bone saw swinging from her belt.
And sometimes it takes more than that.

POEMS, LIKE PETS, DESERVE NAMES

Mary had a little lamb.
Most of us did. We may not cherish
the moment, we may merrily
dismiss it, foment insurrection
in its name, infect introspection
with a body anointed in archaic
oils, look for ways to marry
our failures to torments or blame --
we may farm out our little
Lamb of Shame, feign wisdom,
forgiveness in Mother Mary's
sacred name, we may bridle
our Bibles as we sidle up
to mangers fairly crawling
with lambs, but one thing
is certain: we are curtains
of filth, we deserve our own
disdain, we forsake the faith
of that little animal's lack
of a name -- we are not
pure, we can never be white
as snow, and we know
we have no beasts, no
lambs, no scapegoats –
none but ourselves to blame.

SUDA MAE COMES CLEAN

Slim and taut,
raw as winter
arms pumping
her breasts bob
over metal washtub –
she does everything
by hand,
bathes her bones
in the same gray tin.

Everybody in town
has seen her naked
washing every stitch
late at night, candle
light silhouette
window in the old shed
behind the shack
her home

Children call her
Old Witch of the Stockyard
her best long gone to the wrong
side of the tracks. In fact,
she is not ancient
barely forty years
her birth in the same hard tack,

half her world -- floors of dirt
a soul too soiled to sweep clean.

Once there was a lover,
No-Nose Pete
until the late train greased him
passed out on the rails,
warm flesh so frail
when judged by cold steel.

Rumors fly about a child
of unholy union, a feral creature,
somewhere in the low hills it watches

as you spy on her after midnight,
scrubbing naked sadness from a sparse
wardrobe, not caring about your sins,
or what price you pay to get yourself clean.

SECTION 7

RURAL ROOTS AND URBAN TRUTHS

THE RICHARD BRAUTIGAN TREE

Nah, I never knew him
really, we just
traveled in the same circles

namely, concentric, systemic
we crossed the country
in the root systems of trees

jumping under the damp dirt,
vein to vein, any old tree
would do, again and again

I overheard him
promise to meet a guy at the whore-
house in Havre, MT, with a Box Elder

maple by the back door – who knows
if he really went, I tracked him once
to his place on the Bay, this was seventy-

eight or seventy-nine, I was just a nut
an acorn hanging from an oak,
peering in his window

he was busy tearing corners
off twenties, flipping them in a wooden
salad bowl, it was fated to be or not

to be a Caesar of sorts, some roughage
to unburden his digestion -- his star
fading fast, these were the times

he was so cold, chilled to the bone
Springhill Mining Disaster kind
of alone, still I would see him

popping out on a weeping willow
in Walla Walla, where they all hated
him even in the good times. He

never stopped punishing himself
for the successful years –
by this time, I could smell it on him

stench of the shotgun shack, he
carried it with him for a year
before the act. In the end

nothing remained but tiny corpses
floating like lettuce leaves in little
birch bark bowls. I hung outside

his window, swinging from that oak
for weeks before they found him,
dried blood caked to his head

like tree sap, sticky and sweet,
a spectacle to behold, nothing
anyone living cared to touch.

HENRY ROLLINS FILLS IN AS WALMART GREETER

Welcome to Walmart
Hallmark cards straight ahead
enjoy your stainless-steel cart
Hey dipshit, put on the mask
and start working out,
get in shape you scrawny bastard
cat litter third aisle on the left

LEARNING FROM KEROUAC'S MISTAKE

An old box car is a library on wheels,
a hobo is the Great American
Experience, wind turning the pages,
tearing the body into a ragged
sacrament, drinking the blood of Christ
from a coconut shell. Every bum

on a track or a two-lane is firmament,
bodies shiver in naked doorways, shirt sleeves
opening and closing their mouths, lips
doing double duty, running end to end

in the end, humans can only open
so far, the final leap must be from star
to star, only their own can hold
their own, mud and cigarettes
taking their place in the cosmos,
cracking up, blinking out

EXPERIENCE IS THE FORTRESS OF KNOWLEDGE, UNDER ATTACK BY THE ARMY OF EXPERIENCE

You grow up
on a farm in eastern Montana,
you know some things
city kids don't know.

You know the reason
not to open both doors
on a pickup truck at the same time.

You put your back to the wind,
blow your nose with two fingers --
wash axle grease from your hands
with dirt, not water.

You know the two ways
to cuss, the one when you joke,
the other when you mean it.

You know how to piss outside,
factor the climate,
how to stand, plant your feet
in fertile soil, when
to sign your work.

You know which direction
a chicken runs when you chop

off the head, you have seen
the life in a dead eye
blind to its own closure.

You kill a rattlesnake with a shovel
or a hoe, you don't shoot at it
with a gun. Better

yet, you pick it up on the end
of a pitchfork, walk it a hundred yards
down a gravel road, set it free
in the tall crested wheat grass,

because life, like water
and truth, is precious out here.
You don't throw away
today, what you might be
thankful to have, tomorrow.

BEING WALKED HOME AFTER A BLIND DATE WITH JESUS

Oh, *Heh Heh and Ha Ha,*
it's a little awkward and yes, it did
get weird, let me catch my . . .
I have to thank You, I had no idea
I mean, that You were *Out There*
I would have thought You'd be *Taken,*
Spoken For
Your visage so dark and somber,
Your olive skin so beautiful –
from the ad I expected a Hispanic
gentleman, of course what matter?
it's just a name, You know;
a name is all it is.

Underneath that amazing sky
(You changed the color of the sky!)
or did You just change the eyes through
which I see? It's not the first time
I've gotten a little tipsy, a little loose
around the rules, I have tendencies –
(did You do something to the water? I asked
for water, but it tasted -)
it all felt like, You know, intoxicating, a sign;
a sign of things to come.

The cold meal You prepared for me,

It was so raw, so delicious

(the fish, it was a new type of sushi? The hard

dry loaves, as if they just appeared in Your hands)

Your hands, Your touch, so strong, so tender

I was blind, You gave me sight

And then – well, after

How carefully You washed my feet,

so gentle, like the touch of an angel –

all so weird, so wonderful,

reminding me of John Lennon and that song

"Norwegian Wood" – do You remember?

Such kindness, to walk me all the way

home – can't help but ask:

May I see You again?

(If I return to Your house on Sunday,

will You be there waiting?)

Will it still feel the same?

IMAGINING AUTHOR'S NOTES ON THE MODERN PROMETHEUS BY MARY WOLLSTONECRAFT SHELLEY, 1818

Painstaking my twists
as I stitch these notes together
like the corpses in the tale I bribe

Incessant rain often confined us for days
Was God monster or fool
to steal fire from his brethren
bestow it upon mortal man
scream when he himself was put to the torch?
Water's reflection a mockery of death
of rotting flesh reanimated
My hideous progeny; I have an affection for it
life force beats inside dead heart of beast
remember IT IS ALWAYS COLD INSIDE
the demon never warms
except when bathed by innocent blood
pathways not to places, not to understanding
out of reach
put to the sword
impaled on blades of ice
When death and grief were but words
anger of seeing the angel inside himself
mother's memory sewn into the man I see
infidelity in the heart, MY heart, MY sorrow

lightning is the stolen fire of tomorrow –

eternal sorrow sat upon his face

sepulcher eyes of children, only characters

of vision in the realm of images

as he bent down and kissed the forehead of the boys

to give oneself the gift of birth

How do I show this to my own beloved?

My Lord Shelley, he fairly orders me succeed

The need to kill the Elizabeth in him

beware for I am fearless, and therefore powerful

head bobs up full, between chapels of ice

declare bride inside the horror

marriage of spirit burned into flesh

ice is a black scrape on the sky

fire is birth to ice is birth to pain

Capture life in dead eyes

Water's dark pathway

What terrifies me, will terrify others

windmills and wagons

wheel on the water at the windmill's mouth

monster steps up like a flight of stairs

Who is the main character in reality?

Life, though only an accumulation of anguish -

How many corpses redeemed by flame?

- is dear to me, and I will defend it

head bobs up in the ice of sacrifice;

shall the dead, unliving, fear pain?

This poem is based on both verified and speculative notations on the original novel, as written by the author of that work.

DID THE YELLOW MATTER? OR, IF IT'S A POEM ABOUT THE BEATLES IT JUST ABOUT HAS TO RHYME

How much will it cost
to blame Yoko Ono?
For breaking the Beatles
all those verses ago

like a ghost with John
at the Let It Be piano
pushing back against Paul
and his pudding pop solos

Wasn't the long, winding road
already split and unpatched,
hadn't the Norwegian Wood
been lit by mismatch?

Spats over a walrus,
dead dog custard dripping
from an eye filled with thunder
or a raven's beak tapping

at Eleanor Rigby's window
her face screwed into a jar
secrets buried in the churchyard
watched over by George's sitar

when a hundred things mattered
but just one reason why
nothing but hell swells below,
above us only sky

SECTION 8

BORN ON THE TILT-A-WHIRL

AMERICAN TILLAGE

Each piece of paper peeled from a wall
lights somebody's cigarette, becomes family
in a purely biblical sense, but entangled
a block and tackle love affair, a snake
in the back seat of every marriage wagon.

Never married, never happy, you fancy
yourself born on a snowy peak in Tibet,
a hirsute white man with purple teeth
living in a rainbow of vaginas. This world,
right-minded, has begun to unravel. I am sick
with the smell of content, I want a new life
in a new place, a glass tank filled with minnows
shaped like cotter keys. A fortress afloat
with well-aged whiskey. I am exhausted,
thirsty, and need to build an empire.

FIVE FICKLE USES FOR PICKLE JUICES

A pickle will glorify brine
as if wine, promote bitterness
as a sip of pure bliss. A pickle
sees beauty in lumps and warts,
supports barely closed sores
like silk purses.

Dill pickle blood jars you, like French
kissing with your Russian stepsister,
it's getting you nowhere
but you travel at cartoon speed.

In cases of ill-conceived sex, use it
to wash the truth from your careless
lies, it tries to tell all
as you take a long fall
from another tall building.

Asleep Sunday morning in your car
parked on the archdiocese lawn,
naked with your pants locked in the trunk,
your mind makes shadows to hide behind –
all the Lord asks of you, is your time.

When all else fails, therapists wait
in the wings, their minds stretch
like rubber bands, so you eat

their chrysanthemums, swallow
pride as if wine was the elixir,
not just a mixture of shame
and blame, in reckless decline.

MOUTH AS FURNACE

My tongue a shovel
piling in cold thought as fuel
for the warmth of understanding
or a pile of pity to burn
poorly, puts off an odor
like meat rotting under floorboards
words used as prisons
hope is the key, it snaps off
in every lock, every time
the attic is flame and ashes

DEAD MAN'S SHIRT

My arm dangled in the sleeve,
lifeless as the namesake
of the garment. "I'll take it,"
I said, but of course it took me.

At the grocery some guy
I did not know called me
by a stranger's name, slapped
my back, too hard to be
a friend. He looked long
into my face, studied features,
said "I heard you had passed"
mentioned a wife left behind.

I punched him then, showed him
fists dead to the notion of mercy,
pummeled him among cumquats,
beat him red with radishes.

When they pulled me from the body,
I caught a glimpse in the vegetable
mirror. The shirt was familiar,
but the face like an alien, reversed --
the rage, anger hanging
from my skull like a smile.

THE DEEP RED BLOOD OF THE PROSAIC

The kettled orphans rattle their spoons --
we hear their noises, and move away
to the far side of the room, to continue
our writing. Their little snarls sound
like the music of old cartoons.

Someone mows the lawn here
every other day. It's about the appearance
of normal, but we all enjoy the smell
of newly clipped greens. Yesterday
a bird fell from a pole, its beak
hanging loose at one corner,
a dissident, fiery words cut short
by the flash of a rifle. Peanut
Butter Guy stood and laughed.

None of us remember
anything. A few still try.
Some believe there are machines
out there, constructs of love
and mercy to guard us, piles
of stripped gears at their feet,
like broken robin's eggs.

NIGHT VERSE

I was painting at a friend's house. The sub floor exposed,
sheet rock primed, plumbing not installed. I had to pee.
I took a nearly empty paint can to the bathroom, squatted
over it. I let the stream commence. Missed the can at first.
Put the lid on afterwards; shook it. Left the unused urine
on the floor. I slept a bit. Nothing disgusting had happened.
A baby crawled by. I dipped my brush in the can and painted
its little lips. The moon crouched like a fist on the horizon.

NOTES FROM THE BUFFALO JUMP

It was somebody else
It was not our stampede
we just wanted to stand back
stand back and stir fry
concrete derby dance
on blocky rocky head
enjoy the stir fry
no need to jump and end
up dead
the bus had no driver
brick on the gas pedal
Funhouse Charlie in the mirror
as we went on, I heard
Jesse ask me, Dad
can I have new teriyaki shoes
when we wake up under this bed

SECTION 9

BEATING THE BUSHES

THE OXPECKER

Its name
so out of place
tiny bird on rhinoceros' back

how many words
heavy on a dead tongue
to reanimate the jaws

which spoke them?
How long the ghost
before it loves the job

there is rhythm
in what is lost,
eyeballs bulging

skulls cracking –
dissolving is music,
it must be kept safe

a bloody hide
this ruined animal
on which we crouch

to eat fleas
from the tailbones
of kings.

CHERRIES

Bring me a cold bowl
ripe and red,
delicious to the eye.

I bow my head;
tears fall like broken mirrors
into the concave.
An ocular drain -- the color,
clear as glass.

The bowl unfolds
its own hue, all the better
to reflect the true.

FINDING WHAT YOU ARE NOT LOOKING FOR

looking at your own face
in the truck's rear view
while your brother's wife
goes down all over your lap
all you can think:
"does my brother look
like this, when this
happens all over the long
and short of him?"

If there is going to be an eruption
if there is a grease rag
under the seat, will there ever
be a time when it is not too late
to reach for it, to feel it out
like a bowl of cottage cheese
in your lap at Sunday dinner
at your brother's new apartment
he looks at you like he knew
all along you had a spider inside
and somebody asks him
"How's the wife?"
as he gazes down at his lap
comes a soft knock at the door

YOUR LOST WORLD

I have seen you there
you walk from room to room
legs as straight and strong as guitar
necks, your conquests all wrecks,
never pristine, ever lonely

your tired dogs are made of devotion
your sweet roads of candy corn
there to break your fall into gentle motion\

glimpses of gandy dancing
romantics poke holes in your footsteps
broken bones are forgiven like envy

One day I will knock on doors
swim seas, maraud in sprawling cars
I will assail your frosty prison,
with jagged hand and jaded vision

your lost world is as real
as the gold dust in your eyes,
as sad as ghosts in your smile

it peels you like an egg
which hates its own shell,
like bones locked inside a star

in truth it is you who is lost,
locked between all the worlds –
you who straddles a loaded rocket
with no fuse, a distant instant

barefoot baby in search of shoes.

GUNS DON'T KILL PEOPLE FAST ENOUGH

Guns don't kill people
guns make wicked love in the shadows of tall buildings
guns cleanse the prostate and sweeten the pot
guns walk the dog in between the lightning strikes
guns sing soft lullabies to blind babies with frozen ears
guns rock.

Guns drive truckloads of moonshine across state lines
guns wear special contact lenses emblazoned with the image of Jesus
guns set the pavement on fire
guns do all the wishing and hoping and praying for you
guns sacrifice virgins under peach trees heavy with fruit
guns never let you down or cheat on you with a friend
guns have advice and money to lend.

I don't shoot people
I turn my gun loose in the back yard
it goes commando and free range, it gallops along the fence line
my gun shoots in between the cracks
the thin slits of light that separate one night from the next
I stretch out in the patio chair with hands behind my head
my gun calls all the shots
it is always straight and true; my gun loves its job
I am just the furniture
my gun is boss.

Guns won't kill me

people will kill me

everyone is to blame for what my gun does

my gun is just a gun

what exactly am I when I hold it, squeeze it tight?

My gun is just a gun

I am the bullet

I am the target

Guns don't kill people

they perforate history

as it strolls along the boulevard

you will never see them coming

guns are loyal like family dogs

guns are inside of us all

our skeletons are made of guns

our brains are bullet soup

everyone is in my sights

and I am in everyone else's sight

it is the beginning of the middle

of the night

aaaaahh . . . guns.

BOILED

"You may have a heart of gold but so does a hard-boiled egg." -Maya Angelou

An egg is the perfect universe
there is only strength in numbers
if the number is one

The symmetry cannot be challenged
yet put the egg on a flat surface
all things being equal
there is ultimately nothing but inequality
perfect flat surface
the egg always rolls anyway
the egg never rolls the same way twice.

To hard boil requires the stroke of twelve
a strong egg holds breath
toughs it out as liquid heats outside and in
responds with a thickening of resolve
pain from pain, or pain
from cessation of same
two fears collide as liquid boils outside
stiffening the yolk by degrees

A hard-boiled egg retains its perfect shape
As shell chips away –

The three-minute egg is a soft boil
uncoils into the abstract
safe but never fulfilled
unstable, and as the shell peels
symmetry is lost

Somewhere between these two
the egg fights to hold its shape as walls fall
is there a regret that the hard boil was never earned?
Relief that it has surpassed soft surrender?

THE GRASSHOPPER AS BUTTERFLY

The grasshopper is a butterfly
from Satan's black cornstalk,
endless -- you cannot kill him
with kindness, you cannot prevail
over this Living Hail. He eschews
consequence for crops he chews.
Driven mad, you may sever his head,
but seven more shall surely rise.
Hard and cold, peace of our world caves
behind armor-plated eyes.

OLD AGE

slow, impatient
I move through the city park
it is autumn, the battleground
with its green face has surrendered
to the gray visage of rot --
too old to walk,
I roll on tiny wheels
a statue of concrete
cold to the touch, colder still
in the chill of the eye.

Wind, my only trustworthy
companion -- above my head,
gulls fill their stiffened wings
with promises, words
of spring -- I no longer
count on or believe in.

Children gather round me
as I trundle on, they beg
by singing songs, laughter
like a mask against my weathered
frown. *Ancient Father*, the boldest one
chirps, *Dearest old Codger*
of the Gods, give us a boat, please
oh please, buy for us a boat!

I angle towards the river. "Instead,"
I say, "I give to you this river,
swim its span a dozen times,
you may grow a set of balls,
with which to build yourselves a craft."

they point and laugh, mouthing
the words, mocking the years –
teasing the earth which gives them
light. I hoist my crumpled fist,
off they run, heads down,
cackling into the windmill blades
of fate. I pull my coat collar close,
bend the brim of my hat –
I wish for the gulls to fly far away,

escape this pillar of decay.
Aloft, they are innocent,
blessed or cursed with another day.

SNAKE RIVER

Better part of two years
roaming the canyon, collecting --
like blowing your nose
on tinsel, wind rustling quiet
in the trees. Always found them
on the bank, inches from darkness,
damp as the breeze.

Was act of shedding a part of them,
as in ritual, habit, a thing
so easy, so eager, no thought
accompanied the squirm,
what sort of gyration,
a rhythm of release,
or a shimmy, a vibrating worm

shrugging it off, seeing it
empty in the rear view
did they slide into current,
wash away the dirt of the dead
pieces of themselves,
take a deep breath, start
fresh and new?

In the bullet of their minds,
what did it mean --
bigger, better, was it

like hunger the morning
after a night of fights?
Take back the world.

I stood for long moments,
dark canyon, silent
on a slippery shore,
I felt my body break.
I tore away my yesterday
hide, found myself becoming --

forgiveness bled across me
like a wave, I felt the glide
cool water, new skin
a gasp of birth, from within.

SECTION 10

THIS IS DEDICATED TO THE ONE EYED

PHIL RIZZUTO

(for Joel Westacott and Ken Callahan)

Phil Rizzuto fielded the ball
threw the ball
Phil Rizzuto hit the ball
he fairly killed it, hit it out
of the park, day games or dark

Phil Rizzuto never snorted coke
off the turgid nipples of a starlet
named Harriet, never endorsed
Aurora model kits of Judas Iscariot

Phil Rizzuto was most valuable player
in the American League, swam
the English Channel in army fatigues,
turned more double plays at short
than a man with three knees

best bunter in baseball history,
went crazy announcing Yankee games
once his playing days were gone,
"Holy Cow!" mistook the full moon
for the Great State of Texas
knew the words to every Beatles song

after ninety years he died,

same day as Mickey Mantle --

twelve years apart, both

laid to rest in Yankees flannel

EILEEN HAS RETURNED FROM THE WAR

(for Berta)

Her long grey jacket shows history's wear;
she is never to remove it again.
She will keep it sewn to her bones
as long as life is alive inside the skeleton of sin.
Crows in the yard swoop over her head --
they unravel with nightmares of her face in their bed.

She stewed and sashayed
pretty thing, silver of buttons and coat
until the war muddied her brow.
Yes, she fought the gnarly Billy Yanks
gave those northern pigs a poke
ate corn pone hot from ramrod's shaft
mice slaughtered in dirt under cover of dance,
left a foot in the smolder
fields of cotton, the killing floor
Eileen comes home old from another new war.

Eileen has battled in so many wars –
scars inside hard to hide in her eyes;
harder yet to heal. The old lady hobbles
with clumsy grace, thin lines hide inside
contour of her face. She goes on,
three good feet to take the missing one's
place. Her grey tabby coat

worn with a soldier's grim pride;
a protector, the rose that cannot decompose
lies at night 'cross her throat.

At twilight when the horrors come back on her,
witch doctors crawl
like rain in her fur
I hold her close, her purr tingles my skin
phantom paw kneads my face
we see cracks in the wind

before scores settled at war
we fill a small space --
her claws piercing my side,
whiskers kissing my face.

DEFINITION OF DREAM

(for ASK)

No one needs it
we all know what it means
"I had a dream last night"
It starts, it goes
we hope it comes again,
or beg for it to end

it is a cold shot in the morning
a spasm in the night
it is an ideal, a pinnacle to reach
for as we fall from a precipice
so steep, it makes us small
so wide, it makes us cry
out with pain and ecstasy
we pray it makes us fly –

a malaise so beautiful
a thrill so hard and empty
we wait for one of us
dreamer or dream
to curl
to die

INSOMNIA NECKLACE

(for Shari)

I dream you in bald sunlight
you wear the sleepless night
like a jewel   cold stone
of unclosed eye
naked against your breast

a shine without light
a memory without regret
just bangles   baubles
raw nudity of language

dressing you up
to sparkle like blue snow –
it drifts about the clear, cold orb
it sees through garden and tomb,
pinch of heat, sliver of cold
the squint of winter's morning

CLOUD PARTY OVER THE BEAR'S PAW

(for Charlotte and Josh)

Where clouds are Yesterday People
wearing coattails of mist and azure,
like their formerly living selves
only congregate for birthdays,
weddings, funerals

In Mount Centennial heavens
every day is all three. Like
breakfast, lunch and dinner
atop a table of stars,
one ushers the next into place
each passing over like a wheel

People are born here, or come
from far off hillsides,
all to worship the beast they find
in their garden, the wind that travels
so long, so hard, it never departs,
never arrives. People love this land

and always will, so long as the land
can love itself. Lay down
your weapons, set aside your anger
rise up with your shovel –
stand tall behind your plough, humble

yourself, as dry grass bows its head --
there is nothing so rich
as Missouri River mud
on a poor farmer's boots.

TRUE NORTH

(for Nelson)

The wind a golden river in your winter hair
like fingers of apple butter on a pancake
sky, the way warmth gathers cold –
captures it from the inside out
no lock or chain holds a loved one
so tight as the mountain braces air.
Fresh from the source
each breath greets your skin –
bounces back with your fragrance,
simple in sound, simple in posture –

above the snowbelt, a mountain
man posed into majesty,
he squints far into the north
revisits the bends your river marks.
He bites hard into a winter apple
feels skin crackle,
teeth reaching deep
to the core:
to seeds, narrowing
to one tiny dark stone
where light excuses itself,
cuts in front of shadow

A TREE SOFTLY TURNING

(for Nancy)

I got the idea from black and white TV,
Wally and the Beav and Ward's scouting
knife, chipping bark from a maple, caught
red of hand, pulled by an ear, locked
in their room, feeling bad, one more year

You, the first-grade crush, blush of maple
syrup eyes -- did not know what to do. Jacked
a knife from Sonksen's hardware store, picked a tree
in the park, stretching high, made my mark
STEVE + NANCY

                      but wouldn't you know,
effed it up, knife blade too large for my hand --
one eye looking out for the man -- slashed so deep
into my right thumb, Y cut too steep, its leg
much too long (tip of the digit still sometimes numb)

Cuts you make around you, flaws you don't fix
even sixty years' growth can't heal all hurt
kind skin grows slowly under winter's cloak

mends pain as new seasons rise --
a stolen blade cleaned,
returned to display -- new life

rings a tree now grown too tall,

to see old wounds behind branches

summered in maple, snow covered come fall

THE SPIT HORSE

(for Cheri)

In the time of bean bag
chairs, we sat naked
in popcorn, high as kittens
of white frosting

watching *Koyaanisqatsi*
copulating as time lapsed
before our world collapsed
like a sliver in your silver eye

A WOMAN WHO EATS FLOWERS

(for Ayesha)

A woman who eats flowers
becomes the flower,
as the flower becomes woman

soft petals blush,
light unfolds inside
where the morning lives
through the day, bright bites into darkness

A woman who eats hyacinth
becomes a beating heart of gold,
skin so soft, cold to refresh,
inundate. An animal

peels its own essence
black, released from Black
giddy with the tingle –
excited with the knowing
whatever goes into woman,

comes out again in bloom,
an absolute caress of lavender

like the soil of the flowerbed
glistening under the fingernails
of a woman who blossoms, a woman

with roots, yet wandering,

endless, alive.

ARROWHEADS

(for Dana)

I was small and growing, he was old
and growing small. He bent his back

walked the restless sands on northern banks
of the Missouri as it reclaimed the land.

A child walking at his side,
I was a gun anxious to fire, a bullet

panting to fly over surface and sky.
He moved slow, eyes on the earth.

"Warriors walked here," he said.
"They fought and died. Their bones

have become sand, but their weapons
remain. Now we take their steps.

Watch your feet. Those people
left history here for you."

Years ahead and now gone by,
I wasted my eye on heavy books,

professors' words in sterile halls –
if only I had listened

as history walked at my side
like blood in my veins,

wind in my face,
voice like tapered stone
to guide my way.

About the Author

"SIBRA" - Found Internet Poetry

Sibra is used at least 180.

Sibra is a privately held company in Toronto.

Sibra is a small town boy from Eastern Montana who grew.

Sibra is known for painting The Artist Auction Records Buy /.

Sibra is a passionate painter of Provence.

Sibra is a brand by company Abraxas doo.

Sibra is largely engaged in Apartments Sibra operates in Portland.

Sibra is a director and writer.

Sibra is on Facebook Join Facebook to connect with Steve Sibra.

Sibra is on Facebook Join Facebook to connect with Ryan Sibra.

Sibra is nicknamed.

Dedications & Acknowledgements

This book is for **Ayesha** – a narrow ribbon of light who binds the darkness in my soul. It is also dedicated to the memory of **Lawrence Byron Green**, 1929-2021.

GIVING THANKS

Many blessings and much devotion has been given to me in my role as creator of this volume. These gifts have enabled me to write the material found on these pages. I will forget somebody. Maybe several. To those, my apologies.

My love and gratitude:

To my loving and devoted wife **Stacey** – without her patience, wisdom, guidance, did I mention patience? Without her – no book. No writer.

To a core group of friends who gave love, support, and guidance (literary and otherwise) – including in no particular order Christian Downes, Erika Brumett, Damian Whalen, Craig Edwards, Roberta Edwards, GG Silverman, Lynne Ellis, Doc and Ken, and no doubt others who should be mentioned here. In a broader sense, a thank you to the writers and organizers of Works in Progress and the other open mics in the Seattle area – thank you.

To my Erka, heartfelt love and gratitude for writing an intro to this book.

Finally, as a small-town boy, a thank you to certain other small-town boys who have befriended and inspired me over the years: Mark Dunlap (Circle, MT), a lifelong friend who is there when I need him, no questions asked. All the rest are from my tiny hometown of Big Sandy, MT.

Jon Tester, the first friend I made in first grade, a person who in over sixty years of friendship has never let me down, not a single time. My cousin Ray Sibra, who on a fall morning in1976 took swift and brave action to prevent a farming accident which would have ended my life. Every breath I have drawn since that day, I owe to him. And to Jeff Ament, no more than a casual friend really, but a man I find, time and again, has inspired me through his words and deeds – to try to be a bigger man, to see humble beginnings as a springboard and not an anchor.

ACKNOWLEDGEMENT OF PREVIOUS PUBLICATION HISTORY

The following poems, which are included in this book, were previously published in the literary journals noted below. In some cases, there have been minor changes made.

- The Stranger first appeared in *One Art: A Journal of Poetry*
- The Letterman first appeared in *Trestle Ties*
- The White Widow first appeared in *Word Lit Zine*
- Let The Jamaican Frankenstein first appeared in *Word Lit Zine*
- The Woman In The Box first appeared in *Coffin Bell*

- Dead Man's Shirt first appeared in *Dead Skunk Magazine*
- Guns Don't Kill People Fast Enough first appeared in the Swallow Publishing anthology *Humans in The Wild*
- Eileen Has Returned From The War first appeared in *Chiron Review*
- Ark was previously published by *Lothlorien Poetry Journal*

Cover design by Craig Edwards.

Front cover artwork by Steve Sibra.

Interior Illustration *Earthbound* by Ayesha Siddiqa Khan.

Back cover photo from the family archives, taken in May 1974 by my mother, Arlene Geyer Sibra, in our family living room. She was proud of her trouble-making only son. He selected such an adorable and charming date for the prom.

Thank you to my publisher, Jennifer, for believing in my work.

One Final Swipe: THE SHOES FOR BABY BONEYARD

Truly as an afterthought, I have decided to either honor or defame (the choice is theirs) these individuals by mentioning them in this book. Over the years of dust and asphalt, these people have crossed my path and left a mark – some large, mostly small, for better or for worse, at their discretion. Some are still around, others are long gone. Welcome aboard, either way – like it or not, you are a part of me somehow. Order here, as in life, is arbitrary and means nothing.

- Mrs. Hashley – in 4th grade told me, "Steve, be as silly as you want to be."

- James Worthington Hastings III – captain of my rudderless ship
- Russ, Ralph, Bub – "Keeeeeeep."
- Sheila Jenkins – Shmeela Shmack on deer skin gloves
- George And Wanda Streby – True Americans. Respect. Always.
- Christine Tester – Telegram Baby
- Jason Beach, Chris Knight – Twin sons of different mothers
- Carmen "Wil" Sibra – the Bulletman. El Taxiola
- Uncle Budd – the monkey wrapped his tail around a flag pole
- David Orson Tester – the John Milton of lyrical dog butt poetry
- Donna Christensen – I had such a giant crush on you
- Kathy Richardson and the Wrecking Crew
- Alfa Sibra – no sugar in the Kool-Aid
- Jack Halter – always saved my bacon and rarely knew it
- George Ament – Unbreakable Comb, Fantastic Four #57 with no centerfold
- Ron Church – a four color frenzy
- David King, David Melvin – San Diego, Oakland, Liquor Barn in Redding
- Pam V., Dawn G. & Kathy M. – Teeth and Face
- Bo Blazek – Failure to correspond to complimentary procedure
- Silent Windmills In The Sky – Dawn Matulevich, Marcia Peterson, Holly Fallon, Kris Beck, Joan French, Diane Cornelius, Shannon Parker

www.ingramcontent.com/pod-product-compliance
Lightning Source LLC
Chambersburg PA
CBHW020253130626
46549CB00005B/2194